ANCIENT STRINGED ◪ INSTRUMENTS ◪

Musical Clues to the Past

by Patti Vyzralek • illustrated by Paul Lackner

Orlando   Boston   Dallas   Chicago   San Diego

Visit *The Learning Site!*

www.harcourtschool.com

Introduction

Searching through a royal burial site in ancient Sumeria, a scientist discovers a beautiful stringed instrument. It is a lyre (līr), last played nearly 4,500 years ago.

Scanning the walls of an ancient tomb with a flashlight, an Egyptian archaeologist makes a similar discovery. She finds a 4,000-year-old wall painting that shows a harpist plucking strings and entertaining his listeners.

Examining an ancient Grecian vase, a museum worker sees a festival singer painted on the surface. The Greek singer is holding a kithara (ki´thə•rə); he, too, is plucking strings to make music.

These ancient stringed instruments, and others like them, are valuable clues to mysteries of the past; they help us understand the important role music has played over the millennia. Scientific discoveries about stringed instruments in ancient Mesopotamia (present-day Iraq, Israel, Syria, and Jordan) tell us much about the lifestyle, rituals, and beliefs of that ancient civilization. So, too, do similar discoveries in Egypt, Greece, Italy, India, and China.

Although many miles separate the countries where these ancient musical treasures were found, there is a relationship between the instruments. They are part of an important human bond—a common interest in music made by vibrating strings.

Knowing about these ancestors of modern-day violins, harps, and guitars helps us understand our own human ancestors. Above all these instruments are proof of common cultural interests that reach across borders and across time.

A Common Love of Strings

Scientific evidence shows that ancient people all over the world played stringed instruments. The evidence also shows that these instruments were very popular. Among the most loved of the ancient instruments were the lyre, harp, kithara, lute, vina (vē´nə), and zither.

What's more, people played these instruments in the same way—by plucking the strings. If we listened to music from these ancient instruments today, their tones might seem strange to our modern ears. Some listeners might even think they sounded hilarious. To the people of the ancient world, though, that music was beautiful.

ANCIENT CIVILIZATION STUDIES

Although people played the ancient strings in a similar style, their instruments did not always look alike—nor were they made of the same materials. In addition, they had different numbers of strings.

The Construction of Ancient Strings

The strings of some of the instruments were made from animal intestines or hides; others were made of silk or plant fibers. People stretched the strings to get a sound. Some strings ran across long necks; others were stretched across a frame. The strings usually ran from a sound box at the instrument's base to an arch or crossbar near the top. The stretched strings vibrating over the sound box—like human vocal cords—created the musical tones.

The bodies, or sound boxes, were made of carved wood, tortoise shells, leather, or even gourds. Animal skins covered some sound boxes. The sound boxes increased the sound made by the vibrating strings.

The shapes of the instruments and their decorations depended on the cultural interests of the civilization. Some were rectangles, some were triangles, and others were oval or round. Some had carved figures as part of the design; others looked rather plain.

The Sounds of Ancient Strings

Ancient musicians plucked the strings to get the desired sound. They did not use bows, nor did they strum the instruments. They did not play them with a flourish. Instead, they plucked the strings slowly and methodically. Sometimes they used their fingers or fingernails to pluck the strings; at other times the player used a plectrum, or pick.

Ancient musicians often played these stringed instruments unaccompanied. People thought highly of these solo performances.

Audiences also loved the gentle sounds made by stringed instruments. The tones helped soothe frayed nerves throughout the ancient world. According to the Hebrews, the sound of the lyre calmed King Saul. Chinese emperors also enjoyed these calming sounds.

Stringed instruments were part of the everyday life of
commoners, too. Sumerian musicians playing harps were as
much a part of the marketplace in ancient Ur as were the
street vendors. An ancient Roman musician playing a stringed
instrument in an arcade or at a festival was not an uncommon
sight.

Stringed Instruments
of Ancient Greece

Stringed instruments were especially important in ancient Greece—perhaps more so than in any other civilization in antiquity. The Greeks sang songs at festivals and religious events. They also sang at family occasions such as births, weddings, and funerals. They sang to the accompaniment of a harp, lyre, or kithara.

Written music of that time does not exist; however, historians know that poets recited rhythmic words while plucking a lyre. In fact, the words *lyre* and *lyric*—which means "poetic words written for singing"—are Greek in origin. Many historians believe that early Greek music was slow and rhythmic.

Learning to sing and to play the lyre was an important aspect of a boy's education in ancient Greece. It was part of his training as an amateur musician. Additionally, a boy used lyre music to accompany his poetry. Some boys learned to play the kithara as well. These boys became professional musicians who competed in contests. The ancient Greeks held winners of music contests in great esteem, much as they did those who succeeded in athletic games. Even warriors and heroes, both real and imagined, played stringed instruments as they sang heroic epics and stories.

1. Grecian lyre
The lyre was the most important stringed instrument of ancient Greece and Rome.

2. Grecian kithara
The kithara was a large lyre with a wooden sound box.

3. Egyptian harp
Arch-shaped or triangular harps were popular instruments of ancient Egypt.

4. Sumerian lyre
A bull's head, an important Sumerian symbol, decorated some lyres of ancient Ur.

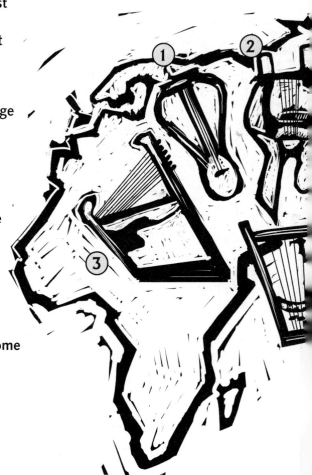

Lutes and Lyres in Myths and Legends

Two stringed instruments, the lute and lyre, play major roles in ancient myths, legends, and folktales. These instruments charmed people who heard them and helped royalty and gods achieve great feats.

5. Indian vina
India's arch-shaped vina was a harp with two gourds at each end.

6a. Chinese zither and 6b. Chinese lute
The zither and lute were favorite instruments in ancient China.

The Victorious Chinese Lute

In "The Victorious Lute," an ancient Chinese folktale, one hero outsmarts his enemy by playing a lute. According to the legend, Kung Ming's enemies were preparing to attack his city. He instructed the residents to open the city's gates. Then he told them, "Don't get excited or frightened when the enemy approaches."

As soldiers came closer to the city, Kung Ming started to play his lute, plucking the strings calmly. He pretended that the enemy was not important. Those around him were getting worried.

"Hush," he quietly told them. "Don't sulk." He continued playing the lute.

The enemy troops started toward the gates, but they stopped and listened to Kung Ming's music. Hearing the music, the soldiers turned away and left the city unharmed.

People in the city were amazed. Kung Ming told them why the enemy had left. "When they saw how peaceful the city was and heard the beautiful, soothing music, they thought it was a trick. They were afraid we would ambush them, so they left us alone."

Kung Ming and his lute were honored as great heroes.

Stringed Instruments in Greek Myth

The lyre appears in several Greek myths. Greeks believed the god Hermes invented the lyre. The legend says that when Hermes was a baby, he sneaked off and stole some cattle from the god Apollo. He used the intestines of one cow for strings and a tortoise shell for a sound box. Apollo complained to Hermes' mother about the theft. Hermes' father, Zeus, told Hermes to return the cows. When Hermes began to play the lyre, however, his music so charmed Apollo that he told Hermes he could keep the cattle in exchange for the lyre. After that Apollo became the grand master of the lyre, playing it to entertain the other gods on Mount Olympus.

The Greeks also believed in stories about Apollo's son Orpheus. Orpheus sang and played the lyre and kithara so beautifully that he could control nature. His music tamed wild animals, caused trees and plants to bend toward him, and soothed violent tempers.

In one legend Orpheus's wife, Eurydice, died and was taken to the underworld. Orpheus went to look for her, carrying his lyre. When he arrived in the underworld, he went straight to the palace to stand before the ruler. He played his lyre before the throne and begged the ruler to let Eurydice leave with him. Impressed with Orpheus's music, the ruler agreed to set Eurydice free, but he also required that Orpheus not look back at Eurydice until they reached the upper world.

Unfortunately, Orpheus was impatient; he turned to look at his wife just as they reached the threshold of the world above. She disappeared instantly, and soon Orpheus died from grief.

Pythagoras Unlocks the Mystery of Strings

Ancient people tried to explain the mysteries of life through their myths and folktales. However, a real person explained to the ancient world the mysteries of pitch and tone, which describe the sounds produced by plucked strings. This person's name was Pythagoras (pə·tháʹgə·rəs).

Pythagoras was a Greek scientist, born about 580 B.C. As a young boy he was a bright student interested in astronomy, mathematics, and music. Like all young boys in ancient Greece, he also learned to play instruments and recite poetry.

One day Pythagoras was walking past a blacksmith's shop. He listened as the blacksmith hit anvils of different sizes. As the blacksmith struck the anvils, each one made a different tone, and Pythagoras wondered why.

He decided to investigate. He experimented with sounds made by stretching and plucking strings of different lengths. Pythagoras knew that when he plucked the strings, they vibrated to create tones, some producing high tones, others producing lower ones. Being a scientist—which was something of a novelty for his time—Pythagoras did some tests.

He noticed that the longer the string, the lower the sound, or pitch, that it made. He also noticed that the shorter the string, the higher the pitch. These observations helped him answer his question about the anvils. The smaller the anvil, the higher the pitch of the tone it made when struck. Likewise, the bigger the anvil, the lower the pitch.

Pythagoras also learned that he could change pitch by tightening and loosening strings. Tight strings produced a higher pitch, while loose strings produced a lower pitch. Musicians today use what Pythagoras learned about ancient stringed instruments to create low tones on cellos, higher tones on violins, and a variety of tones on guitars.

His interest in numbers led Pythagoras to discover what we now call musical octaves. Imagine plucking a string on a guitar. Then imagine placing your finger at the halfway point on the string. If you hold your finger there (at the halfway point) and pluck the string again, you will notice that the sound of the string gets higher—by one octave. When Pythagoras did this, he saw a relationship between a numerical musical scale and the length of the string. His inquiries into music led to what we know today about tuning our modern stringed instruments, such as violins, cellos, and guitars.

How Greek Lyres Were Made

Making lyres was a highly valued profession in ancient Greece. Craftsmen who made them earned great respect.

Choosing a good tortoise shell—tortoises abounded in ancient Greece—was a lyre maker's first step. The shell became the lyre's sound box, or resonator. After hollowing out the shell, a lyre maker stretched a strip of ox hide around it and covered the places where the turtle's head and legs once stuck out of the shell. Then he attached wooden horns to the top of the sound box. Next, he placed a crossbar between the horns at the top. He tied seven strings to the crossbar, stretched the strings across a bridge connected to the tortoise shell, and attached them to a tailpiece to finish the lyre.

Making a Model of the Greek Lyre
Materials you will need:

- 1 sturdy empty cereal box, at least 7 to 8 inches wide
- Scissors
- 2 pencils
- Tape
- A single-hole punch
- A wooden ruler
- 7 rubber bands that can stretch to at least 6 inches
- 2 cardboard tubes at least 5 inches long. (You could use 2 cardboard tubes from the center of toilet paper rolls, or one center tube from a roll of paper towels, cut in half.)
- Crayons or colored markers

Directions:

Hint: *You will be turning the box inside out to make the lyre.*

1. Turn the cereal box upside down. With your fingers, carefully loosen any glue holding the box closed. Open both the top and bottom ends.

2. Find the long seam inside the box that holds it closed. Gently loosen the glue holding it together. Spread the opened box out on a flat surface. The bottom of the box should be facing away from you.

3. Locate the two largest panels on the box. Starting with the right-hand panel, cut out a large U shape at the edge. *Leave at least 2 inches on each side of the U shape.*

4. Using the piece you just cut as a pattern, trace a similar U-shaped piece on the large left-hand panel. Cut out the piece.

5. Refold the box to form the sound box of the lyre. *Make sure the printing is on the inside.* Join the side seam that holds the box together. Tape the seam closed.

6. Fold in all of the bottom flaps. Tape the bottom of the box closed.

(Directions continue on Page 16.)

7. Use a paper punch to make 7 holes under each U shape for attaching the strings. Punch out the holes at the bottom edges of the U shapes. *Make sure the holes are at least $\frac{3}{4}$ inch from the edges.*

8. Fold in the flaps at the top. Fold under the right- and left-hand sides first. Then fold the other flaps down and tape them shut. The box should have slit-like openings on the top right and top left edges.

9. Push your ruler through one slit at the top of the lyre. Loop the rubber bands over the ruler. Push the ruler through the slit on the other side of the box.

10. Carefully stretch each rubber band down to one of the holes at the base of the U shape on the front. Starting on the right, pull a rubber band through a hole on the front, then on the back, then loop it over the end of a pencil. Move the pencil a little to the left and thread another rubber band onto it. Keep moving the pencil to the left until all strings are looped over the pencil.

11. Cut 4 slits, evenly placed, around one end of each cardboard tube. Spread the flaps of the tubes out. Tape them to the top of the lyre as the "horn pieces." Decorate the lyre's sound box to look like a tortoise shell. Use art materials to make the horn pieces look like wood.